"You're Going to Ride an Elephant on Friday!"

And

Other Things They Didn't

Teach Me

In

Principal's School

By

John K. King

"You're Going to Ride an Elephant on Friday!"

First Edition

First Printing, 2011

Cover design by John Morris-Reihl

Proof-reading & editing by Marty Hale

ISBN:

Copyright@2011 John K. King

Printed in the United States of America

Table of Contents

Introduction

You're Going to Ride an Elephant on Friday and Other Things You Didn't Learn in Principal School

This book is for those of you who are thinking about becoming a school principal or for those of you who have always wondered what a principal does all day.

My "official" training as a school principal was excellent! I learned about school law, special education, education finance (oxymoron), how to manage a school that has a 2 million dollar budget, how to evaluate teachers, and how the public schools work. I learned a lot, it was hard work and I felt I really earned that degree.

It did not prepare me for how the job really works, what can happen on a daily basis and how you sometimes just have to laugh at what is happening around you.

I had to learn how to work with a close-knit community. I had to learn how to handle getting in trouble for making the right decision.

I had to learn that you may be asked to do some really interesting things to show that you are "pro" the community and "pro" the kids that come to your school.

I had to learn to be a painter, a plumber, a psychologist, a coach, a mentor, an advocate and a better listener. I had to learn to laugh at myself and situations that came my way. I had to learn how to handle things that come a principal's way every day.

I had to learn to be a principal.

All the stories in this book are true and they occurred during my first 8 years as a principal. I was young, green and totally unaware of what I was getting myself in for.

It was worth it! I love being a principal because every day is different. It's just that some days are more different than others.

To those of you reading out of curiosity, thanks for reading. To those of you who are training to be a principal, let me tell how it is really going to be for you.

John K. King

September, 2011

An Endorsement for this story:

As a former school administrator, teacher, and coach, I take this opportunity to weigh in on the work of John King, the author of this short, but funny and significant piece of prose for any newcomer to school administration or even the more experienced administrators.

This book is filled with heart-felt stories and reflections of one man's experiences with people, places, and local culture. John King shows extraordinary courage and honesty about the past experiences of a professional career, as he conveys the intricate tapestries of the schools and their cultures as seen from his vantage point as principal or assistant principal.

All of us who have worked as school administrators have the cadre and collection of stories that depict the true character of the people who define the communities and cultures surrounding and embracing the schools they claim as their own. None of us were truly prepared for the work to be done. Not in any textbook was it written that one might have to referee a near fight between two board members, or become the counselor to adults and children over the loss of a staff member, or hold and comfort a child who lost a parent, or buy food and clothing for kids and their parents who are homeless and broke. The mere

7

act of showing that level of love and concern and commitment is what defines us all who choose to work as school administrators. We, after all, know all the details of every back story, where the teachers and other staff only get the headlines. It's not an issue of us and them, but rather a variation of the role one plays in the orchestration of the part of child's life we call "school."

In this short, but immense piece of narrative, John King lays it all out. You will laugh. You will cry, but more than anything, you will have a better understanding of the role of a school principal. It's not about the power of the position; it's about the people you suddenly can affect.

Happy reading!

Dr. Jesse R. Hale

Chapter
1

I had grown up and gone to school in the Northern Virginia Area. This megalopolis has the largest number of people in the Commonwealth and therefore has the largest school districts you will find anywhere.

I attended Fairfax County Public schools and attended a local college – George Mason University. My goal was to be a band director in the same county and be looked up to as a good musician, director and teacher. At the tender age of 21, I didn't realize that kind of success would take years of hard work, dedication and a little luck. I graduated in 1979 with a Music Education Degree and I began my teaching career as a band director for several parochial schools.

I also got married in 1979 just a few months before my 22nd birthday. So I was young, newly married and I needed a job, any job. So I signed a contract for $9,000 a year. It was more money than I had ever seen in my life. I had worked part-time jobs throughout high school and college but that paid only minimum wage. Now I had a real job and was making real money.

In 1980 my son Matthew was born and in 1983 my son Jason was born. So in 1984 I decided with two kids and a mortgage that I needed to make more "real" money and I took a job as a general music teacher in the Fairfax County School District. I first worked in several schools each week helping the main teacher with their overflowing classes. I enjoyed it and learned a great deal about teaching and kids. I learned that you should not play drums loudly when you are using a boiler room as a classroom. People just might think the school is going to explode. I also learned not to let the Emotionally Disturbed class play with rhythm sticks. For some reason they didn't want to play rhythm. They wanted to beat the crap out of each other – and me!

Luckily in 1985, my principal at Clermont Elementary, E.J. Whitley decided to increase my time there and I became a full-time music teacher. For the next five years, I became more involved in every facet of the school. I became the Safety Patrol Coordinator, The School Council Association Advisor, and I volunteered to help E.J. as much as I could. I liked her and I wanted her to be proud of me and my work. I also loved everything about being at school. I loved being there and helping out and I learned a lot about curriculum and people.

During this same period, I separated from my wife, moved into an apartment and began taking courses that I called Principal School. It seemed with child support, (which I never missed a month), and rent I needed to make even more real money. I had decided to go to Principal School because I found being involved in every facet of a school fascinating and exciting. (At least it was never dull!)

In the summers of 1988 and 1989, I completed my internships as a principal of a summer school. I was basically free labor and I was there to do everything a principal usually does in a miniature format. I had to take care of kids and talk to parents and make sure the summer school staff,(that was paid), had everything they needed. It was a great learning experience.

In 1990, I completed my Principal Schooling and in the fall of 1991, I was appointed the Assistant Principal of Silverbrook Elementary, also in Fairfax County. I had the amazing opportunity to work with Ms. Yvonne McCall. She was a regal African-American woman who loved to wear purple. We would all be worried when she started a conversation with, "Yesterday when I was taking a bath, I had an idea…." This usually meant work for me and the teachers to make the "idea" come to life. It was an amazing school with over 1200 students and some of the best teachers I have ever seen. They cared about the students and they cared about each other.

In May of 1991, I married my best friend Patricia and we moved to Fredericksburg Virginia. Now this was an hour away from where Patricia taught middle school math and it was an hour and a half away for me. However, we wanted a place that was ours and nowhere near our first mistakes. For the next few years, we made the daily commute up and down Interstate 95 going through tires and windshields like normal people changed their oil.

In the spring of 1993, I decided that once again it was time to make more real money and I applied to our neighboring school district, Prince William County. It wasn't because I thought I was ready to be a principal or I was tired of working with Yvonne. The truth is, my child support went up and now with a new wife and trying to blend a family, it would be an easier endeavor if I could make more money and be in charge of my own building. (So I thought.)

I was invited to a panel interview and when I entered the tiny room, I thought there was no way in Hell I was going to get this job. There were 21 people sitting in a tightly made horseshoe of mismatched tables and chairs. I had learned in Principal School that more than 7 people in an interview could be a disaster. So, I felt I should have been given a cigarette and a blindfold prior to the first question. I decided at that moment that I would just answer the questions as honestly as possible and use it as a learning activity.

I was invited back to meet with the current Area Superintendent late one evening later that month. He was packing up his office because he had taken a job in Washington State. It was just a bit disconcerting to know that my possible hiring would be one of the last things he would do – if he hired me. He explained that he had a small elementary school in the western end of the district. The school's present principal had resigned and it was in need of a new energetic principal who could work with the parents. The school, Nokesville Elementary was built in 1929 and it was an important part of the local community because the parents and their parents had attended there. It had 350 students mostly white, country folks.

I told him I could do the job, (although I was scared to death). He said he would make the recommendation for me to be hired at the next school board meeting. The following Thursday night, Friday morning actually, I received a call at 2:00 a.m. that I had been appointed as Principal of Nokesville Elementary. I was excited, nervous, and still scared to death.

On July 1, 1993, I officially became the principal of Nokesville Elementary School in Prince William County, Virginia.

Now my training formally began!

13

Leadership Lesson #1

The undergraduate and graduate training you receive is important, essential and wonderful as you prepare to be a principal. It is designed to train you about educational law, finance rules, special education requirements and how public education works. The training begins your life as a scholar. You have to continue to read and study and learn about the job.

Your biggest training will be on-the-job training. You cannot read about how to deal with situations and parents and teachers and the latest educational fad. You cannot listen to a lecture about how to fix a dangerous bus stop or how to help a poor family or a child who needs glasses or who grieves the loss of a parent or grandparent.

You will learn by doing, listening, remembering your mistakes and thanking God for your successes. Most importantly, you must make an effort to grow in the job every day.

Chapter

2 [i]

Where the Heck is Nokesville?

Now that I had my first principal job, I had to find out where this place was. The interviews were all done at the central office and I thought there was no need to go find the place and then be told I didn't have the job. Now that I was appointed, knowing where I worked seemed an important thing to know.

I have the worst sense of direction since Wrong Way Nelson. I can get lost going home. I asked Patricia to help me find this place and to see what it looked like prior to July 1st. Remember, this is before websites and I didn't know what the Internet was yet. We found our map, got in our car and went to find Nokesville.

We traveled up Interstate 95 and took the Route 17 North exit. We traveled 45 minutes to route 28 also known as Sudley Road. We traveled east for about 10 minutes until we came to the town of Nokesville (a good sign). We took a right on Fitzwater Drive, and entered small town America. There were several antebellum homes, a post office, the Church of the Brethren, and a railroad crossing. We crossed the tracks and on the right sat a grand old brick building with a big Nokesville Elementary Sign out front. (Must be the place.)

As we got out of the car to walk around the school, we noticed the farms located behind and around the school. We could see the Blue Ridge Mountains in the distance and the large trees that had grown between the 3 trailers and 2 outbuildings. They provided shade and beauty to the foreground.

The school itself looked every bit its age but it reminded me of the school I attended briefly as a child, Stonewall Jackson School in Alexandria Virginia. There would be a large multi-purpose room with a stage as you walked in the front door. There would be classrooms located all around the multi-purpose room. I was sure about it but I couldn't prove it because I couldn't get into the building. I had not been given the keys to building yet.

I know I looked like a kid looking through the ground floor windows into my first school but I had to. It was my first school and I was going to have to do everything by myself. With only 350 kids or so, I would not have an assistant. It was just me. I couldn't wait to get started.

It only took an hour to go from Fredericksburg, a Colonial city to small town America. I loved it. I couldn't wait to get inside the building to see what it looked like. I also couldn't wait to trim the overgrown bushes out front and add some curb appeal.

Too bad I wasn't able to get into the building and begin my first year as a principal until late August 1993!

Leadership Lesson #2

No matter how long you work as an administrator or in the field of education, never lose your enthusiasm for the job. Go to work every day feeling like the kid looking through a candy store window.

No matter how hard a day or week might be, remember how you felt when you got your first job; when you were anticipating your first day. Not only will it give you more energy, it will energize the people around you.

Most educators/principals will tell you that their work is a "calling". Never forget the feeling of the call. It will help you get through the tough days and make you appreciate all the days.

Chapter 3

Asbestos – The Floor Show

The biggest thing in my favor as a brand new principal was I had no idea what I was doing. With only two years of experience as an assistant principal, I had more hubris than I had knowledge. What I lacked in understanding I made up with energy, humor and a willingness to listen to other people.

During my walk around the school in that late June afternoon, I failed to notice a huge pile of plastic that was located in the back of the school near the cafeteria. I had no idea what it was for but I was soon going to find out.

After signing my contract and getting the keys to my little kingdom, I was told that I could not get into the building. It was being tented so they could contain the asbestos that was located in the floors and underneath the stage. During the interview process, I failed to ask a question about asbestos in a 64 year old building. I failed to inquire about the last time renovations were made to that old, regal building that I had only seen from the outside. I was beginning to wonder if some of the outbuildings were outhouses but I couldn't check because I wasn't allowed anywhere near the building.

I was told that all the files and information about the school had been moved to a room at Brenstville Middle/High School located down the street from my school. So, on July 1, 1993 I drove to Nokesville, passed my school, (I waived as I went by. It did not respond.) and parked in front of Brenstville MS/HS. I was greeted by a man wearing a golf shirt, shorts, and a large straw hat. He was holding a golf club. This was the affable principal of Brenstville. He welcomed me to the area and to the town and then went on to talk for the next 30 minutes seemingly without taking a breath. The principal told me about how close knit the community was and how I was only the 7th principal Nokesville has had in its 64 years. He said people come and usually stay a long time because of its teachers and kids and because we are so far out people leave us alone.

I liked the sound of that.

He led me to my room in the main corridor. It smelled musty and moldy. I had a typewriter, (Yes a typewriter.), and boxes marked simply Nokesville stacked up all around the room.

Now July 1993 was probably the wettest July I had ever experienced. It seemed to rain constantly for days. This would not have been a problem if my room at Brentsville had not leaked like a sieve. It seemed as Nokesville was getting some needed renovation, Brentsville was in greater need of a new roof. I spent days emptying trashcans of water and replacing them under the several leaks located just in my little room. It seemed that our buildings were far away from the maintenance department too.

Although feeling like a mushroom because I was damp and in the dark, I used the time to read as much as I could about the staff and the school. I read the curriculum, looked at past yearbooks, looked at class lists and began to get an idea about our clientele and our stakeholders. The only diversity we had was in the teaching staff. We had three African American teachers and about the same number of African American students. Our diversity was economic diversity. Nokesville had one of the smallest enrollments in the system but had a huge attendance zone. We would be served by ten to twelve buses. Some of the buses had 20 kids on them and others had only a few.

A brief aside about our bus drivers: Many of our drivers had been driving for years. They had driven the parents of our present students to Nokesville. So, they could take care of discipline problems long before they came to me. They would park the bus and knock on the front door of the house and tell the child's parents what a jerk their child was being on the bus or at school. The parents usually would take care of it. It was wonderful! I gave my drivers good Christmas presents every year and another gift at the end of the school year. It was money well spent!

The other thing I did while I was waiting for the building to be cleared so I could actually see the inside of the building, was invite the staff in to meet with me so we could get to know each other. I asked everyone two questions: "What are you looking for in a principal?" "How can I help you do your job?" Almost to a person each one said: "We want you to support us and be fair." "We want you to listen to us when we have a problem or a solution to a problem." I felt from the beginning that it was a good staff that had been through tough times recently and they just wanted be allowed to teach their kids. Since I was still trying to figure out what I was doing, I was happy to have a strong faculty around me.

Finally, in early August, maintenance called me at Brentsville and asked if I would please come over to Nokesville for a meeting about what they had been working on. I took the 30 second ride over and finally was allowed to see the inside of the building.

"Maintenance" had taken the last month to put a new sub floor on the existing asbestos tiles and then re-tile all the floors. They also covered the area below the stage that was used as storage. It would not be allowed to be used for anything anymore. They just closed it up and sealed it tight. The term I learned that day was friable. The asbestos had to be covered so tiny particles of it couldn't fly through the air and get into people's lungs. It occurred to me that everyone had been breathing it for the past 64 years, but it was a good thing it was being taken care of now.

You would think the asbestos story would end there and I would be moved into my office and begin my career as a principal but you would be wrong. The problem was that the floor didn't stay down! In the span of two years we would end of getting the replacement floor replaced.

The first sign that there were problems was when we would see tiles sliding past us as they slid down the hall. This became a daily impromptu game of shuffle board. Tiles would be kicked by students and adult accidentally and on purpose as the problem became more acute. I actually began to give points for distance and accuracy as they slid down the hallway either toward the office or toward the multi-purpose room. If the tiles were still in one piece, we would put them back and try to glue them back down. Even if those stayed down, others would take their place. They would stick to our shoes better than the sub floor and we were tripping over them.

The second sign was when a group of maintenance workers came in to look at one of the hallways and made the pronouncement that, "The tiles aren't straight." I told them I wasn't as worried about them being straight as much as I was about them being low flying projectiles. Even the roaches were becoming alarmed.

They decided that the entire floor had to come up and be replaced. I told them it wouldn't be hard to remove the present floor, I could get the kids to help them and the kids could have souvenirs of their time at school. Maintenance decided to do a section at a time to make sure that the glue was right and the floor was straight.

As a result, the final floor turned out beautiful. It took a little time to get used it because with the sub-flooring, thick glue and thick tiles, the floor was now higher than what we were used to. We would trip going up the stairs for months while we were getting used to the height of it. It looked like we were drinking on the job.

During this floor adventure, I was taking an inventory of the inside of the old building. It needed a lot more than just flooring. The old plaster walls had been painted but it was now peeling in the humidity of the summer. The one faculty bathroom in the main hallway needed an overall just to be presentable to the teachers. The front of the building still needed a great deal of trimming and pruning.

I was not going to ask maintenance to do anything else but maintain their focus on the floor. I would have to do the other work. I did not mind. The old building deserved to look better and it would look better, if it ever stopped raining.

Leadership Lesson #3 – Learn baby, learn

The first priority after taking over a school is to learn about its history, its background, what is important to the community, the established traditions. You will be surprised how important traditions are to any school community. Some have made Halloween the biggest celebration of the year. Some have made the homecoming dance second only to the prom. Some have made the school a focal point for the Apple Blossom Pageant or Harvest Festival. By knowing what is important on the calendar will help you become part of the school.

The second priority is to know your people. How long have they been there and what is important to them. If you know the school traditions and the school faculty, you will make the best decisions for them and the students.

That is ultimately why you are there.

Chapter
4

Painting, Flags and Touchups

As I got to know the old building, it became apparent that the paint that they used on the walls during the renovation did not agree with the plaster walls. It was pealing constantly. I began to walk around the building with a paint scraper, a brush and a dust pan. I would see a spot, scrape the loose part off, clean it up and then come back with a paint brush and cover it.

I would scrape everyday and the staff would laugh because I was trying to get every little spot every day. I tried dry wall paste. (Doesn't work on plaster.) I tried some other things that also didn't work. The walls would reject it like the paint and I would come in the next morning and have a huge part of what I had done laying on the floor. It looked like the school had thrown up. I began to think that the school was laughing at the new man.

After all that work which was done in an effort to make the building look better than tenement housing, it ended up looking like.....walls that had been scraped repeatedly and painted over. The dark side of the moon was smoother than my walls.

During the summer 0f 1994 I decided to tackle the auditorium's 20 foot high walls in an effort to improve its look. (Obviously I had been breathing in lead paint.) I enlisted my youngest son to help me with the endeavor. We climbed our ladders, scrape a section, painted over it and moved down and started again. We slowly did the entire auditorium. It took almost three days. Afterwards, we both realized that the walls looked like the other walls. They were better but they looked like old plaster walls that had been scraped and painted over and over again.

So I had to come up with an idea of how to take the spotlight off the walls. I decided to purchase flags representing 20 countries from all over the world. My son Jason helped me put them up straight. (Cannot see straight either.) On the right wall we began with the American Flag. On the left wall we began with the Canadian Flag. (We figured our students would at least recognize those two.) We then spaced them out all around the auditorium. It created a different visual focus for the wall and I had to admit….It looked great!

In the next months, I would purchase cheap framed art works and add them around the hallway walls in an attempt to cover up the worst cracks, flaws and over scraping. With the new floors and new walls, art work and flags, the place was beginning to look like a school. I was not sure how many countries our kids could identify by the flags hanging around their auditorium. So I put a laminated sign underneath each flag identifying each represented country. Unfortunately, the signs wouldn't stay up on the walls. Every morning I would find several lying on the floor of the auditorium. The next morning, there would be different ones down. The school was playing with me again. I finally took them all down and threw them away.

I still had to scrape and patch and repaint, but I only walked around once a week to check the walls instead of everyday. My staff had to find other things to laugh at me about.

I learned that as a principal I had to care about the how the building looked. It couldn't have bad walls and paint peeling off the walls and bad floors. It was a school. It was where learning was supposed to take place and any place that you expected kids to be needed to look the best it could. Otherwise, kids won't think what they do is important or what is expected of them necessary. Kids, parents and teachers should see that you care enough about them to care about the look of the building too!

A coat of paint, a few paintings and 20 flags did make a difference.

Leadership Lesson #4

Never underestimate the power of paint and cleaning supplies in your hands. Do not delegate every cleaning job to someone else. You will receive more respect and understanding when the community, staff and children know that you care enough about them that you work to help keep the building looking as good as possible.

Take the opportunity to paint a wall, hang a picture, pick up dirt or empty a trash can. You are the caretaker of the building. You need to be the care-giver as well.

Chapter 5

You're Riding the Elephant on Friday!

In the fall of 1995, the circus came to town. It wasn't Barnum and Bailey but it had erected a large canvas tent on the grounds near Brentsville Middle/High School. We had received fliers advertising the circus. The students were excited about it and even the parents and teachers were discussing what day this weekend they were going to go see the circus.

This circus had the usual tigers, lions, jugglers, clowns, cotton candy, trapeze artists and elephants. It had several large elephants.

The day before opening night, one of the circus' managers came in to the office and asked to speak to the principal. I came out and shook his hand and he told me that an important tradition of the circus was to have important people of the community ride an elephant into the big tent to begin the show. He wanted me to ride the elephant on opening night!

I was honored at the request. I was humbled. I couldn't believe that a third year principal of a little elementary school would be asked to ride an elephant into the circus. I was taken aback. I was a complete idiot.

I realized later that this was a brilliant ploy by the circus to get more people under the tent to pay admission and watch the show. I realized later that it was not for my celebrity or hard work that I was chosen for the honor of riding a very large pachyderm. I also realized later that I had the honor because most of the political figures and important members of local society said, "Hell no!" when they were asked to ride an elephant into the circus.

My staff and the kids thought it was great and I immediately began to get mentally prepared to ride an elephant. This is not something you can practice. You cannot go to the local zoo and say, "Can I borrow that big gray one over there for a while." My goal became a quest to not look stupid, to not embarrass myself and to not fall off the damn thing.

So on opening night I drove over to the circus and met up with the genius who talked me into this and we went over how this worked. He told me that the elephant in question would bend his front legs and lean down and I would climb and sit behind his head on a sort of blanket that was tied around his neck. I would ride in to the main tent where I would be announced and I would wave and pretend that I was having a good time and then I would get off the elephant in the same manner that I had mounted him and then go and watch the show.

It sounded so simple I knew it wouldn't work.

At around 6:30 p.m., I saw a young man walking with the tallest and biggest elephant I have ever seen. He was actually quite beautiful and he walked with a slow deliberate walk. (What did I expect, a scene from Fantasia?) The animal stopped and immediately under the direction of the handler, lowered his front section so I could grab on and sit on his back right behind his head. Now this was a good deal wider than I had imagined. I thought I was going to look like John Wayne sitting on his palomino. Instead I was sitting wider than I thought a man was intended or physically capable of sitting. There were muscles that I had not used in years now barking in fear and agony. I did not want to fall off and embarrass myself and probably die in the process.

The elephant and I began to move slowly and for a brief instant I felt like I was something else. People were already waving as I made the ride toward the tent. Children were laughing and pointing at me. Teachers were taking pictures to prove that I was stupid enough to do this.

As we came closer to the tent, I was thinking that this wasn't so bad. I showed that I was a good sport and that I could tell all my peers that I had rode an elephant. Then it became clear to me that the handler had forgotten to tell me that the opening of the tent was slightly lower than the height of the elephant. The main cross pipe holding that portion of the circus tent was right at the level of my forehead! I would have assumed that the height of the elephant and the height of the rider would have been included when erecting the opening of the tent that same elephant and rider would be entering. However that was not the case.

It became apparent as I got closer to the opening and closer to the exact moment when people would be either waving and applauding or praying and calling for an ambulance that I would have to do the limbo as I entered the tent. I tightened all my muscles of my legs and butt and prayed that I would not get knocked off the animal and I leaned as far back as I could just for as long as it took to get passed the metal pipe. I could see it as it passed within inches of my face, glasses and forehead. I immediately popped up and started to wave and smile at the audience. I know I had the look of, "I meant to do that." on my face. I got off the animal as fast as I could and shook the hand of the handler and walked around the tent in an effort to get my legs to work again.

The circus was fun, the kids had a great time and later in the week my picture astride the elephant was in the local paper. At the next principals' meeting, many of my peers told me that they were impressed that I had done a thing like that. They said they would never do it, not in a million years.

I learned that sometimes your students and staff have to see you take a risk and do something different. I learned that as a principal you have to be part of the community and that means supporting the circus that comes to town, and being present at special events. I learned that elephants were hard to ride and easy to fall off of. I learned that you cannot take yourself too seriously, since nobody else does anyway.

A few years later, the circus came back to town and again they wanted a local leader to ride the elephant. I declined, but the new principal at Brentsville Middle/High took a turn. I didn't go the first night; it would have been too scary!

Leadership Lesson #5

Your job as a principal is not just to be a leader of a school, you are considered to be a community leader too. You have to take the time to be a judge at a county fair, toss the coin at a football game, be a Grand Marshall at the parade, and yes, ride the occasional elephant.

It is all part of the job. It is all part of being a good principal. You represent the school and the community every time you shake a hand, judge a contest, ride in a parade, or attend a sporting event.

Remember, you are never off duty!

Chapter 6

It was only a downdraft!

During Labor Day Weekend 1996, I received a phone call from Campus Police that I needed to get to the school. The school had apparently been damaged by a severe storm the day before. I left immediately.

It was a Sunday morning and school was supposed to start on Tuesday. As I drove into the parking lot on the right hand side of the building I saw some tree limbs down and some debris lying on the ground. There were several maintenance trucks parked in the back and numerous people walking around the building with their hands in the pockets and serious looks on their faces.

As I got my bearings, I began to look past the fallen tree limbs and notice a tree that used to be standing tall between two out buildings was now lying down between the buildings. It would have to be cut up and removed. The amazing thing was it didn't fall on either building and they seemed to have only cosmetic damage.

I continued to walk around the back of the building toward the gymnasium which seemed to be the focus of most of the people who had made the trek from central office. The gym had been renovated just a few years ago when they had removed or covered the asbestos and painted the building. During the renovation, they had also put a new floor down on the gym, and built a new art room off the gym. The original art room in the building had been turned into a computer lab during the same renovation. The art room off the gym was complete with heavy tables, drying racks, and a brand new kiln.

The maintenance crew motioned for me to open the door to the art room from the gym. As I opened the door, I saw blue sky and no art room! The entire room was gone. The paper was seen in different patches as far as two farms over, the tables were gone, the chairs were gone and the kiln was gone! It looked like a bomb went off in the middle of this cinder block room.

For once in my life, I was speechless.

It seemed that the storm damage went from several farms near the school, hit the gym, knocked the

37

tree down, crossed Fitzwater Drive, damaged a silo on the neighboring farm and then headed east toward Manassas. I had never seen anything like it before and I have never seen anything like it since.

As I was marveling at the destruction, I noticed one of the neighboring farmers walking down the parking lot toward us. I could hear him whistling and see his head shaking back and forth. He came toward me and shook my hand, looked up at me and said, "Must have been a downdraft!" Downdraft, I thought, Downdraft Hell...that was a tornado! It was lucky that we didn't lose more equipment or even more classrooms and thank God it didn't happen when kids and staff members were there.

The biggest challenge now was that school was starting on Tuesday and we had two days to make the school look like something and ensure that the students and staff felt safe. The maintenance crew was amazing. They got rid of the tree, cleaned up the area. They put a tarp over what was left of the art room and we took part of the gym and created a temporary art room with tables and chairs and several schools in the area donated art supplies for us to use until our new stuff arrived. They also checked the entire school from roof to basement to make sure everything was safe and there was no invisible damage to the building. On Tuesday, the buses arrived, the kids came in and the first day went off without a problem!

Although local farmers and neighbors would bring to the school pieces of cinder block and other treasures from the old art room, the kiln was never found! A new art room was built with new shelving and tables and chairs and a new kiln. It was ready by the spring of 1997.

I learned to respect weather in all its forms. I learned to be grateful that some things happen when no one was there. It would have been frightening to have something like that happen when students and teachers were in the building. I learned to rely on your maintenance team to get the job done and ensure the safety of the school. They did a great job and I am thankful always for the job they did to help us open on time in 48 hours.

Thank God it was just a downdraft; a real storm would have really made a mess!

Leadership Lesson #6

The first thing you do when you are in the position of cleaning up after a natural disaster like this is thank God that it didn't happen when the kids were there. Storm damage is never a good thing, but happening during a three-day weekend so the facilities could be checked prior to the opening of school made it safer for the kids and saner for the adults.

This also should bring home the importance of emergency drill planning and practice. Many schools do a few fire drills a year and talk about what to do in an emergency. As we know from any educational endeavor, if we practice it enough, it becomes routine and safety routines can save lives when a downdraft does occur during school time.

Chapter
7

L.P. & B.P.

I had the luxury of working with several wonderfully talented teachers during my 8 years at Nokesville. One of my first grade teachers, Lisa Lowe, was a loving, hard-working, funny teacher. She had a great sense of humor and a sincere dedication to her students. Best of all we would make each other laugh almost daily. We would both find the humor in everyday activities and in what students said and what parents and teachers did. It made the workday fun.

Ms. Lowe was also very short, (befitting her name Lowe), and I am over six feet tall. One morning as she came in the door, I noticed she was moving a little slower than normal and she looked tired from the day before. I asked, "You okay?" She responded, "I am just a little pooped this morning." I said, "Well, if you are a little poop, I must be a big poop!"

From that day on we called each other L.P. and B.P. Our peers would try to figure out what the letters meant and we even told some of them. They wouldn't believe us. They thought it had to mean something more mysterious and enigmatic. Nah! It was just two people trying to make work as enjoyable as possible.

I learned that a principal had to lighten the load sometimes and use humor to provide support and understanding. You cannot just be the authority figure who is walking around being serious with important things on your mind; with the weight of the world on your shoulders. You have to make people see the humor in things, walk with them, laugh with them, show them that you are human and that you don't take yourself too seriously.

Recently, I received a phone call from Ms Lowe. It had been 10 years since I left Nokesville. She called to see how I was doing and to give me an update on her retirement and what other former co-workers were doing. She still called me B.P. and I still called her L.P.

We still laughed.

Leadership Lesson #7

Never take yourself so seriously as a principal that you do not laugh, make fun of yourself, or make a co-worker feel better. Just like a principal will ask his teachers to know the kids and know when they need a hug and when they need lecture, a principal needs to know his teachers and offer a hug, an encouraging comment, and especially a laugh.

A joke or a laugh can alleviate stress, show that you understand the challenges they face and let them know that you haven't become less human and less understanding because you became a principal.

The longer you are in a leadership position, the more you will see the importance of laughter, especially laughing at yourself. Besides, they will think you are not as large of a B.P. if you do.

Chapter
8

Dumpster vs. the Retainer

In the spring of 1997, as I was making my daily rounds in the cafeteria at lunchtime, a little boy came running up to me in a panic. He had tears in his eyes and was shaking. I calmed him down and asked him what was wrong. He said, "I took my retainer out to eat my lunch and I put it on my tray, and I threw my tray away, and they told me they have already taken the trash out! My parents are going to kill me!

I asked the kitchen staff and Mr. Herman if indeed the trash had already been taken outside to our dumpster. Of course, it had. I calmed the young man down again and told his teacher that he was coming with me. We walked to the front office to get two pairs of rubber gloves and then started walking toward the dumpster.

I grabbed a trash can and several bags on the way and at one point the little boy looked up at me and said, "Are we really going to get into the dumpster?" I told him, "We aren't going to get into the dumpster but, we are going to have to go through the bags to find your retainer, unless you have a better idea." I could see on the boy's face a combination of awe and disgust.

I informed him that we are going to go through each bag one and a time and he was going to help me move the contents to a new bag in the trash can. Then we would move that back behind us and then go to the next bag. My hope was that it would be in one of the bags near the top. You can be assured that the dumpster was full of bags, and it was a lovely aromatic spring day in the mid-eighties.

As we were going through each bag, several people passed us going from the parking lock to the main entrance. Not one person asked if they could help us in this important endeavor; not one. It took us several bags but finally my little friend announced, "There it is!" He looked relieved and as I looked at the remaining dozen or so bags that had not been opened yet; I said a short prayer of thanksgiving.

My little friend thanked me several times as we walked to the restroom, washed off the retainer and placed it in the plastic case where it belonged. I had a friend for life but I just reminded him that it is okay to get upset when things happen but it is equally important to find a solution to the problem. He looked at me with a "whatever" look and went back to class.

Several teachers asked me why I didn't ask the custodians to do it or get some other people to do such a gross activity. I told them the kid came to me for help and you can't just farm that off to someone else.

A few days later I received a letter from the child's parents. I thought it would be a letter thanking me for dumpster diving. However, it spent more time stating that the school should do a better job of making sure kids didn't throw their retainers away so this kind of thing wouldn't have happened in the first place.

I gave the letter a "whatever" look and threw it away.

I learned that to be important in a child's life you sometimes have to get your hands dirty. You have to do the right thing and show kids how to deal with adversity, hardships or a just a screw-up. I learned also that you do the right things whether you are thanked or blamed. It doesn't matter. You do it for the kids and not for a thank you.

Leadership Lesson #8

No matter what title you have in a school and especially if you are in leadership, you can never think you are too good or too big to do something. If for nothing else, do it for your credibility (school cred.). However, you should do it because your biggest responsibility is to lead by example.

Are you a leader that isn't afraid to get their hands dirty or do you believe you need to delegate everything because you are the principal? Are you a leader that believes that you need to show kids that you care for them prior to asking them to care for each other or do you believe that is their parent's job? Are you a leader that believes that little things and little actions can make a big difference in the life of a child, or do you believe that it is not in your job description?

I look at it this way: Being in a dumpster looking through trash on a hot day trying to find a retainer is not something you want to do. However, it does make the everyday parts of the job look a lot better!

Chapter 9

Walkathons and Walking Trails

One of the traditions that I was established long before I got to Nokesville, was that every April our counselor, Ms Lanham, would coordinate our yearly Walkathon. Every class would come out and walk around the building several times to make money for a chosen charity or raise money to purchase new equipment for the playground.

With only 350 students, our budget was not large and we didn't make a great deal of money through PTA fundraisers or appeals. For some reason, the Walkathon was the highlight of the spring. Everyone enjoyed walking around the entire building and fields. They enjoyed doing something different. I even brought my dog to the event.

48

My black Labrador retriever, Kingdog (I didn't name him.) came with me to school on Walk-a-thon Day. The kids would take turns walking him and giving him water. He was really good with the smaller children. He would walk right beside them as they went all the way around. The bigger kids would get pulled all the way around. He knew the difference and the kids didn't care.

One early spring day in 1998, Ms Lanham, my counselor came to me with an idea of creating a smoother walking surface on the field. She wanted to create a walking trail around the perimeter of the field. It would start at the edge of the right side parking lot go all the way around until it ran parallel to the gym and finish connecting to the left side parking lot. This would create a large area for the walkathon. It would be paved or concreted in the front and the sides of the building and the walking trail itself would be graveled or mulched.

I thought it was a great idea, but I didn't know how it would be done. Ms Lanham had already talked to several of our dads who worked construction or who had earth moving equipment. They had agreed to come on a Saturday morning at 7:00 a.m. and make it all happen.

A few Saturdays later I am driving to Nokesville at 6:30 a.m. to give my input to the Nokesville Walking Trail. When I arrived at 7:00 a.m., the dads had already scraped the dirt that would become the trail and had already put down mulch on 50% of the trail! I was surprised! They must have been there since 6:00 a.m. The dads just told

49

me they had a lot of volunteers and everyone wanted a turn at the adult sized Tonka toys, so they had scraped the dirt, moved what grass there was and then a dump truck would follow with a load of mulch and then another truck would come and smooth it over. They were done with the trail by 10:00 a.m.

Over the next few months, the PTA purchased a Gazebo to sit adjacent to one of the turns of the track. It was big enough to hold over 20 students. We also added little benches and wild flower beds, bird houses and bird baths. It looked great and the biggest expense was the Gazebo that was ready-made and came off a flat bed ready to be used.

The school is still enjoying the Gazebo and still hosting a Walkathon every spring.

I learned that no matter how small or larger your school is your parents have skills and knowledge you may not know about. These parents can make things happen quickly, efficiently, quietly and legally. They know how to do things that won't injure themselves or volunteers. They know how to get things delivered and moved and scraped and beautified. Why? Because they love their children and the best way for dads to show that they do is to build something, move something or get something. That way whenever they see it they feel like they made a difference;

they helped in some way; they used their skills to help their child.

All we needed to do was ask the dads and they were happy and proud to give their kids and all the kids who attended Nokesville a safe and enjoyable place to walk, sit and learn. Not bad for a little school out in the western end of the county.

Leadership Lesson #9

Never underestimate your parents or parental help. They are just waiting to be asked. With the more challenging curriculum, some parents feel that they cannot help their children with the school work they have to do. Fathers especially feel that they are working a lot and cannot go to every meeting or every parent conference. What they can do is build something, install something, improve something, and help create something on a weekend.

When you allow parents to help build a dream, they can always say, "I did that." "I supported my school by doing that." It makes a greater connection between the community and the school and that is always a great thing.

Chapter 10

Leader of the Pack

Every year during the cold month of January, Nokesville held auditions for our annual talent show. We held the auditions after school for several weeks to eliminate inappropriate songs with gyrations or just gyrations without the song, comedians who were not funny and/or musicians who could not play. We narrowed down the amount of groups because it had become so popular, the talent show would begin around 7:00 p.m. and we wouldn't lock the doors and thank the parents until 11:00 p.m.

As the talent show evolved, it would have the normal cute little kids dancing and singing, parent teams reliving their past, parents and teachers reading original poetry, and girl groups doing the Macarena. (Remember that one?) The teachers had to get involved too! (Of course.)

One of our best conceived ideas was a skit based upon the 50's song Leader of the Pack. We had one of our young teachers wear a poodle skirt and put her hair up in a bouffant and act out the beginning of the song. I came riding a tricycle in a leather jacket and my hair slicked back. Every time the crowd heard the "vroom, vroom" of the motorcycle in the song, I would pretend to rev my tricycle.

I rode around the stage two or three times which as you can guess would become rather uncomfortable in several areas of the anatomy. Finally, the song reached the part where he Leader of the Pack had the accident. When I heard "Look out, look out, look out, look out", I pulled the tricycle gracefully to a stop and teetered over like the guy on Laugh in. (Remember that one too?)

Now in rehearsal, several fellow staff members were supposed to come on the stage and carry me off as the music ended. However, when we did the real performance, they decided to bring in rolls of gauze and wrap me up like a mummy. There I was lying on the ground and then I heard hysterical laughter as 10 people came out and wrapped me up in about 20 seconds. If it had been a rodeo they would have won the roping trophy.

Because we hadn't rehearsed this little ad-lib from my staff, they failed to realize that wrapped up, I am not easy to move. At this stage in my life I am about 180 lbs and now that is dead weight on the floor and I cannot move because of the gauze tied around my entire body. My co-workers are also having trouble picking me up because they are laughing so hard. Being the resourceful group that they were they decided to pull me by my legs and drag me off the stage! Luckily as I started moving off the stage the song ended with the final "vroom-vroom" and I was able to lift one of my hands up to rev my imaginary bike looking like this was part of the plan all along.

It was a big hit! We tried every year to come up with something even better but it never happened. (But we got close.) I got soaking wet when we acted out the song Car Wash and I sat in an imaginary car. I was an old Disco Dancer to the tune of Jive Talking. I was the Native American when we sang our version of YMCA. It was always fun and it showed that we could have a sense humor.

I learned that you needed to give kids and parents and teachers a chance to laugh and let their hair down during a cold and long winter. I learned you needed to be part of the group and it was not disrespectful to be the center of a joke. I actually gained respect because I was part of the team and I enjoyed the joke. (Although it did hurt when they pulled me down the stage stairs.) I learned that parents and kids need to see you as a real person and not above them or more important. I learned

55

that we always needed to screen the possible acts because people would suggest strange things...like a 38 year old riding a tricycle!

Leadership Lesson #10

In this age of Common Core Curriculum and threshold testing you would think talent shows and funny skits would have gone the way of dodge ball. However, if you ask your PTA or your older students if they would like to be in a talent show, they would enthusiastically say yes.

A child learns a great deal in school. They learn to read and to cipher and get along with their peers. They learn that passing a threshold test will ensure that they will go on to the next grade. They learn that stress is not relegated to the over 20 crowd.

A child needs to also learn that a school is a place where fun things can happen. A school can be a place of silly skits, adults being silly and where we can have our own version of American Idol.

As a student, I participated in donkey basketball games for charity, took a pie in the face from the kindergartners. As a principal, I have taken a pie in the face from kindergartners, been sank (several times) in a dunk tank to make money for the PTA and even dance on a very hot roof when our kids read more books than the year before.

This is not fluff; this is the real stuff that makes a school a real place of learning and living.

Chapter 11

Mice, Meeting and Testing

As the only administrator of the building, I had to be in charge of everything. One of those responsibilities was as test coordinator. Twice a year, (once for the ITBS = Iowa Test of Basic Skills and again for the SOL = Standard of Learning Tests), I had to make my room into the testing office. I didn't have an extra area that I could house the tests and I didn't have a vault to secure them. This school was built a few years before vaults and testing offices were a standard item. I placed skinny tables on two walls of my office and I placed plastic bins carefully either on the table or underneath them depending on what grade level it represented. Each plastic covered bin had a tag on it labeling the teacher it belonged to and how many tests were in each bin. First grade was on one table and second grade neatly stacked on the floor under first grade. The next table had third grade on top and fourth grade underneath. Fifth grade had its own area stacked neatly between the filing cabinet and the book cases. In short, there wasn't a lot of room for anything or anyone else in the room. However, on that particular fall morning here we were having a meeting in my tiny, test laden office.

It was a special education meeting and it included me, the mother of the child, a special education teacher and my social worker. There are four people sitting around my tiny little table in my tiny little office and I am the only male amongst them. As we were discussing the individual education plan for this child, I notice something moving near the wastebasket located between the aforementioned fifth grade tests and filing cabinet. It was a small brown mouse that decided to see what was going on. He got up on his hind legs and gave a look of, "What's going on here?"

I decided it was not a good idea to tell three female adults in my tiny room that there was a mouse staring at them from near the trash can. I did not need to have my staff hear loud screaming coming from my office. I also couldn't do a thing about the mouse right now with my guests in the room. I also had an office full of testing. I couldn't just throw something at him.

I had to wait.

After the meeting, I walked calmly to my head custodian's office and asked Mr. Herman if he had any mouse traps. He asked me how many I needed. I figured with the postage stamp I had as an office two would be enough. I placed some peanut butter purchased from the kitchen on each trap and placed one trap near the trash can and the other one in the opposite corner of the office.

In less than 2 minutes, I heard a loud "SNAP" and then another "SNAP" coming from the both sides of the room. I now had to clean out the traps and set them up again. I went out to visit some classrooms and when I came back I had to clean them out again. By the end day, I had cleaned them up and reset them 4 times and had dispatched 8 mice to rodent heaven.

This was October and with the first chill in the air, many of the local ratites were coming in to stay warm. Unfortunately, they had selected my office/testing office/vault to settle. It was a perfect place with 20 bins of testing materials, the 5 boxes they were originally shipped in (and would be shipped out in), and my usual files and principal junk. With the testing, I just couldn't cohabitate with my mice friends. I probably would have dealt with it even my office was open, airy and comfortably roomy. Some things you just can't live with.

One of my staff members suggested we get a cat. I told her no. I didn't want to have to explain how the mouse guts and blood got on test booklets and I am sure they would have put the litter box in my office. Why not? Everything else was in there.

I learned that it was important to embrace the responsibilities of the principalship. I learned a great deal about testing, confidentiality, organization, and cleanliness. I also learned that a little school located near farms where they cut the hay in October as the weather was getting colder, could expect mice.

I kept a jar of peanut butter in my office. Occasionally, I would even eat if for lunch.

Leadership Lesson #11

When you work in any large building, you have to ready for anything and everything. Mice are not the only thing to be prepared for. You have to be ready for roaches, stray dogs and cats and even an occasional stray kid. (It happened this year...two younger siblings decided to take a mile walk to visit their sister who was in first grade. They walked all the way to school by themselves. We walked them back home.) We have even seen parents in sleepwear walking their children to class and parents who were inebriated driving their kids to school.

You have to be ready to calmly take care of situations like this without disrupting the lives of the students or the adults that may be around.

No one knew what I was doing except my custodian. I didn't want to alarm my secretary or my bookkeeper. Besides, screaming and education really don't go well together.

Chapter 12

Golf and the Best Weekend of My Life

In the spring of 2000 my PTA officers came to me with a new idea to make money for our little school. They asked if I could approve a golf tournament. It would be a shotgun start tournament and we would get sponsors to provide prizes while it advertised their particular companies. There would be several competitions within the tournament including closest to the hole, lowest score by an individual, lowest score by a team, highest score by an individual, highest score by a team, etc. After checking with the usual authorities, we decided we would do it.

The PTA board said that in one day we could make as much money for the school as a month long fund raiser.

Our fall fund raiser had given us $7,000 that year so if we could get anywhere near that amount, it would be worth the work.

Now I am not a golfer. I believe in the Mark Twain quote: "Golf is a nice walk ruined by a little white ball." I can find other ways to embarrass myself that are much cheaper. (Like riding an elephant.) I did know that planning for something like this was a major undertaking for the PTA and I would support them as much as I could.

Our PTA board was amazing! They lined up the sponsors and the freebies and the golf course for a Friday and got the foursomes signed up and we were ready to roll.

I was asked several times during this preparation whether I golfed or not. "No." was always the answer. Their reply was always, "I can teach you." I knew enough about myself and sports that they could not even with the laying of hands and deep prayer prepare me in a few weeks time to play 18 holes of golf in one day. I would either embarrass myself or end up spending an incredible amount of money on golf equipment and clothes to look the part. Nah!

What I did agree to do was to be the judge at the Closest to the Hole Competition! I was a genius. It was a par 2 hole and all I had to do is sit in a chair wait for the golf balls to land and keep track of the person who was closest. They didn't have to make the putt. I just had to get the right name to the PTA board by 6:00 p.m. that evening.

So I sat in a lounge chair on a beautiful sunny day that was not too hot or too cold and I sat there drinking adult beverages. (The cart came by to check on me every 30 minutes or so and I HAD to support their work as well.) By the time 2:00 p.m. rolled around I was about as happy as an adult male could be.

The only stress came when some of the younger golfers decided to use their Big Bertha drivers on the par 2 hole. When they yelled "fore" I needed to be ready to get bombarded with incoming projectiles that were closer to the next hole than the one I was responsible for.

The winner of the closest to the whole competition was a teenager who landed a perfect iron shot. The golf ball landed 4 inches from the hole! No one did it better and the young man never made a better shot all day long! I was happy for him. The more experienced golfer weren't, but I was.

At the end of the weekend the PTA announced that for one day's work, we made $6,000 dollars! It was a lot of work and a lot of fun and we made a lot of money for a little school with a total operating budget (non-salary budget) of $10,000. We used it to refurbish our walking trail and front garden areas and left money in the PTA accounts for the board next year.

We had a great time and it was the most fun I have had during a fund raiser in my career. I had a headache the following morning. I must have gotten too much sun.

I learned that sometimes you have to let your PTA board try something new. We needed to check to make sure we could do it but we didn't let the complexity of it or the newness of it change our minds. We were able to coordinate a golf tournament that helped the golf course, helped the PTA, helped the school and helped the community.

Where else can you go to raise money for your school and support a beverage cart?

Leadership Lesson #12

Sometimes as a leader it is best to get out of the way and let other people take the lead. They can and will do a better job. You don't give up your authority by letting other people do something better than you can. You don't show weakness by allowing others to show their strengths.

I wouldn't know how to coordinate and manage a golf tournament. I wouldn't know what to do to line up the sponsors and make it a day that is enjoyable for people who like hitting a white ball while taking a long walk.

I do know how to sit and enjoy the blue sky and the green grass and a beautiful day. At the end of the day they thanked me for allowing them to pull this off. I thanked them for their leadership and for their gifts.

A school is a community of leaders and workers. We are workers all the time and leaders some of the time. That is what makes a school special.

Chapter
13

There's Bats in the Gym

Throughout my tenure at Nokesville, we had several visits of bats in the gym. It was rural myth when I got there but it became really true the longer I remained.

The visits were not determined by weather, change in seasons, leaving a door open, losing or rebuilding an art room, or any other reason we could find. A few days each year, we would get a frantic P.E. teacher sending a child to the office that would quietly state, "The bats are in the gym again."

I would call maintenance and inform them of the biannual visitation. I would hear the usual long sigh on the other end of the phone and eventually a group of workers would come out and look in the gym and say, "Yup, the bats are back." They would then discuss how they would capture the little things and return them safely to nature. Occasionally, they would send an exterminator who would come and do the same thing. (I guess he was giving the maintenance crew a break.) I never watched what they did or asked what they did. I didn't want to have to break the news to the students. I would say, "I don't know what they are doing in there. They won't let me in there."

My students were actually worried about the bats. They were, to a child, animal lovers. They would bring in frogs, toads, birds, stray dogs, cats, bunnies, goats, sheep and squirrels. It was not uncommon for kids to come to me during a fall or spring afternoon and state, "The cows are on the playground again!" I would have to go out and look to see what kind of cow it was. If it was 1200 pound Long Horn steer, I could pull it by the horn and take it back to its home adjacent to the school. If it was 300 pound Black Angus, I had to call the owner to ring a bell so they would go home thinking they were going to be fed. Even though the Long Horn looked bigger and meaner, the Black Angus would take a piece out of me and I wasn't going to die by bovine.

The students did love animals and that is good. They learned to take care of each other because they learned to take care of animals. They learned to respect teeth, nails, horns. They learned to realize every animal – two foot and four foot have them.

During fifth grade graduation in 2001, I saw a young man who looked nervous as he stood there waiting to process into the gym and gather his diploma and ready himself for sixth grade. I thought it was graduation jitters. I went up to him and asked him if he was alright. He looked at me and said, "I don't know what to do with this." He opened his hand and revealed a very tiny baby bat that he said had fallen from a tree outside the fifth grade building. I held out my hand. He gave it to me. I walked to the back field behind the gym and held it upside down until it grasped a small limb and hung down and wrapped itself in his wings. I was glad it didn't bite me since there was a full moon that night.

I wondered later if the maintenance people spent as much time hanging their bats up. I decided to leave that question unanswered and went into the gym for the graduation ceremony.

I learned that every school has its own peculiarities based upon its location, its students and its community. I learned that kids know a lot about things and learn a great deal by taking care of animals and sharing what they know about them. I learned that I could drag a Long Horn steer without reprisal, but a Black Angus I am never going to mess with. It is not the size of cow in the fight but the size of the fight in the cow. I learned that even though we could never figure out where the bats came from, it was okay. Our kids would eventually take care of them.

Leadership Lesson #13

The first thing you should do as a new principal or school leader is find out the history of the building. Every school has a history and has a story to tell. Schools are living and breathing edifices and it will make your job easier if you know every nuance a building can have.

I have been in buildings that have "hair-trigger" fire alarms. They go off if someone walks by them quickly. I have been in buildings where squirrels want to go to kindergarten so bad they chew throw the ceiling so they can look into the room and when the kids weren't there, they came and stole the popcorn brought in for snack. I have been in buildings where the power went off so often we never left our computers without saving what we were working on.

You can find yourself working at a school that is connected to a sewer system or you may find out you have the largest septic tank on the east coast and it lies directly below the football field. (The greenest grass you have ever seen.)

You can also find yourself with a gym full of bats and you take care of it and wait until the next time. It is part of the history and legacy and part of its future.

Chapter
14

No, You Cannot Be a Mad Obstetrician!

The other big tradition I inherited when I came to Nokesville was Halloween! Our mascot was a tiger and our colors were orange and black so, why not? The kids were excited as the last week of October arrived. All the parents and teachers and I would try to decide what we would "be" that year. I was a sheriff one year, a clown one year, (more believable), a Star Trek officer, and one year I dressed in a huge sleeper with feet. We had great fun.

During the week prior to Halloween, the PTA would prepare the upstairs area as the Haunted Hallway. Our upstairs consisted of a large library, three 4th grade classrooms and a fourth classroom used for Special Education Resource. During the first part of the week, the parents and staff would start piling up black rolls of plastic, black drapery, scary masks, things that went boo, audio-visual equipment, bowls, cauldrons, costumes, etc. During this week we also had delivered about 20 "art doors". These were two doors hinged together so they would stand up if they made a "V" and usually they would be used to show off students' art work. We used them to make the haunted hallway into the scariest thing this side of the Blue Ridge Mountains.

The PTA board, parent volunteers and I would arrange the boards beginning in the library; connect them by screwing in 1x1 strips of wood so they wouldn't fall down if a child or adult got so scared they hit something as they ran out. (I am not kidding.) We would then cover them with the black plastic or cloth and then we would start arranging the scary faces, lights, cauldrons, audio-visual equipment, etc. Our goal was to make it even scarier than the year before.

The other rooms were used for scary vignettes like Frankenstein, Dracula, guys wearing hockey masks wielding a chain chaw, etc. These were made even scarier via the use of strobe lights, scary music and hands coming out of nowhere provided by students and parents who wanted to add to the eerie.

We had done such a good job in making the Haunted Hallway as scary as possible that the Nokesville/Brentsville Police and Fire Departments came early on the Saturday before Halloween to check it out

73

before we could allow kids and parents to go up there. They usually loved it and only once did they tell us, "No real candles...Move the dry ice farther back...Other than that...it is scary as Hell!"

With their seal of approval we opened around 6:00 p.m. on the Saturday closest to Halloween, scared the living daylights out of people for hours, and then had to clean it up and be ready for school on Monday. So all of it had to be taken apart, stacked up, bagged up, vacuumed up and transformed back to a school. I would get home about 2:00 a.m.

It was a great success. The only challenge I ever had was from one very enterprising and creative dad who asked me every year, "Can I be the Mad Obstetrician?" He went on to say that he had all the gear. He had the scrubs and the big knives and the lights and he even had a surgical table with the stirrups. (I don't know why and I didn't want to know.) He would ask every year and every year I would say no. He was very disappointed but I had to draw the line somewhere.

I explained to him that we had our entire upstairs turned into a haunted hallway where we warn students under 10 that they are going to be scared. We have parents and older students taking great enjoyment out of scaring the younger students or their own children. We have bowls of spaghetti used for brains, we have strobe lights and chain saws and people grabbing on legs as they walk by. We have tombstones made with our names on them. (Mine was most popular.) We have to have the local fire department check it to make sure we aren't shut down for using more power than the rest of the city. We have a great time and the kids and parents love it, but, you may NOT be the Mad Obstetrician. I didn't want to have to explain that to the mothers who were here doing most of the work!

He said he understood. He said he would ask again next year.

I learned that traditions are important and they bring the community together. I learned that it is okay to try to improve it and make it better every year. I learned that it was safer to involve the local police and fire departments than try to hide stuff from them. I learned that it is okay to say no to something that was even too over the top for me.

I didn't want to be the one placed in the stirrups!

Leadership Lesson #14

Sometimes as a leader you have to be brave enough to say no. It is not a fun thing to do and usually it is not accepted well. You have to be willing to offer some suggestions for how you will allow something to go on but within limits of safety, sanity and lucidity.

It would be very easy to say yes to everything and let everyone do what they wanted to. It would be easy to let the PTA make the haunted hallway scarier every year and let the blood flow. However, there might be some bloodletting after the event if you do.

Whenever there is a school sponsored event, you as a principal will always be held responsible because you have the authority. The responsibility-authority connection is never broken. We cannot acquiesce our responsibility and say, "They wanted to do it."

Sometimes for the sake of all, you have to say no.

Chapter
15

Do You Have a Basketball Program?

In the fall of 1997, one my parents came to me and asked if he could use the gym after school to allow the kids to play basketball. It wouldn't be a league and it would only have kids playing against each other. It wouldn't have trophies or anything like that. It would be designed to give the kids a way to get some exercise during the cold fall and winter months. I told him I would check with the upper echelon.

Sports are always big in small towns. My students played sports all year long with the recreation department. They signed up for football and soccer in the early fall; basketball in the late fall; baseball in the spring. In fact, we had to send our performance schedule to the recreation department so we didn't interfere with their games so our kids could attend the performances at school.

In an effort not to get in trouble, I contacted Mr. Mercer at Operations. He asked me if they would be playing against other teams. I said no. I told him the kids would be shooting around and playing against each other. He asked me if it would be open to both girls and boys. I told him yes it would be. (I hadn't told my parent that yet but, it would be open to everybody.) He asked me if we were going to charge any fee to participate. I told him no. (Something else to mention to my parent.) Mr. Mercer told me I could open the gym so that my kids could have the benefit of this program.

Everything was running fine and the kids seemed to be having a good time, until I received a call one morning from my boss Faye. She asked me in a very serious tone, "Do YOU have a basketball program?" I answered, "What do you mean?" She repeated, "Do YOU have a basketball program?" "Yes. I have kids shooting basketball at night. It is sponsored by our PTA." After a short silence Faye responded, "You are not allowed to have a basketball program." I told her how the PTA came to me and then I contacted Mr. Mercer and he said it was okay and we weren't competing with other leagues or with the recreation department...it was just something for our kids to do. Faye was not happy but she did hang up.

A few days later, I received a letter of reprimand from Faye stating that we should not have our own basketball program and that I did not follow the proper protocol and that this letter would be placed in my personnel file. I wrote back explaining again that I took a request from a parent to provide something healthy for our students, I checked with Mr. Mercer at Operations and he said it was okay. I stated in my reply that I did not approve this until it was approved by Mr. Mercer. I also asked that my reply be placed in my personnel file.

For the next several weeks, other letters would come from Faye repeating the same issues. I would reply in kind with my same responses. Finally, one day Faye came to see me and as she walked in she said, "Can we have a truce?" I replied, "You stop writing, I'll stop writing." I even told her, "You even made my bookkeeper cry!" She said, "I didn't mean to. The recreation department was upset."

The AHA moment had occurred. I finally realized that the people at the recreation department saw our little program of about 50 kids a threat to their program when we didn't have a league, there wasn't any trophy, and there were just girls and boys on coed teams playing 5 on 5 during the cold months in Nokesville.

We ended up keeping our basketball program for several seasons. As long as we kept it to ourselves, it was not seen as competition to the recreation department. The recreation department is still not happy.

79

Truthfully, I liked Faye and we only disagreed about a few things but this was one of them. It took me until I was a lot older to learn to keep my immediate supervisor happy at all times. Right now I was fighting for my kids and against the idea that we were trying to be better than the recreation department. Our gym was 50 years old. It had bats in it and therefore guano. The bathrooms were enough to make anyone run away at night.

A few years later Faye retired and called me to say goodbye. She said she enjoyed working with me and that it was always interesting and exciting. I wished her well but I did ask her if she would put it in writing and put in my personnel file. She laughed and got off the phone.

Leadership Lesson #15

You can never go wrong by providing something good for your students. That doesn't mean you may not get some heat from the upper echelon or even get written up. I had no intention of being at odds with my superiors. I don't do that. I know that is a no win situation. However, I do believe in providing the best programs for your students.

My students at Nokesville lived in a rural area. They were kids of working class people who could not drive to the nearest town and pay the fees needed to participate in a recreation department basketball program. I decided that it was a good idea for my students to be able to get some exercise during the winter months with an intramural type program.

I even asked permission before I did it however this was a case of, "It may have been legal but there will be some political payback." I really didn't know that the recreation department would cry foul and think that we were trying to usurp they program. I really looked at it and thought it was different. They didn't see it that way.

So I took the responsibility of the program and what came with it. If I had to do it over again, I probably would but I would have talked it over with Faye too.

Live and learn.

Chapter 16

That 70th Show

In 1999 I decided that Nokesville needed to celebrate its 70th birthday. Some people asked me why I didn't wait until the 75th. I really felt that I wouldn't be there in 2004. Patricia was seriously thinking about retiring and we would be moving to Savannah Georgia if that happened. I wanted to be here when we celebrated being the second oldest school in the system.

As in all things related to a school celebration, some people wanted a big thing and some people wanted something a little more subtle. I wanted to recognize the people who had made an impact at the school: the former principals, the former and present teachers and the community that had supported her for 3 scores and 10.

We invited all the former principals who we knew to come and speak about their time at Nokesville. We asked some former teachers to speak and then some community members to close. Then we had time to walk around and through the building to reminisce and see the changes that have been made in 70 years. (Like 3 layers of tile, 5 layers of paint, pictures and flags on the walls, the tile flooring in the gym that replaced the real wood one which had rotted away in the 70's, and nobody was going to mention the asbestos.) Our final destination was the library, where we would have light snacks and finger food.

It was a simple yet a very successful celebration. The superintendent made a short visit but spoke to the audience of about 100 people. One of the former principals came and spoke and said that he always remembered Nokesville as the "best time of his life." He had been Nokesville's principal for 15 years and was glad to be back. Each speaker said how they were proud of the school's history; proud that they went there; proud that their children and grandchildren went there.

When it was my turn to speak, I thanked them for what they had brought to the school. The community is what makes a school. The parents and children and teachers and neighbors and alumni and well-wishers gave Nokesville and every school their heart and soul and energy and life. I thanked them all for being part of the school and being part of the celebration. We all crammed together for pictures and then we began the grand tour of the grand old building.

It was during our tour that the group really became animated. Many grandmothers and grandfathers shared stories about former teachers getting on them for doing something wild like climbing out the second story window and dropping to the ground. They all had different opinions about why the storage area was called the dungeon. They shared hilarious vignettes about Halloween, haunted hallways, Christmas Trees catching on fire, and the how the gym was haunted with a ghost of a little girl in a red dress. Later I just walked and listened as the mothers and fathers shared more recent tales and heard some present-day students sharing what happened last week. It was simple, fun, and historical. It was living proof that the school had made an impact for several generations. It was wonderful!

I learned that sometimes a celeb ration does not have to be too extravagant to do the job. I learned that people came to celebrate what they already knew: Nokesville was an integral part of their lives, their community and their family. It was family. They came to celebrate all the teachers and students and administrators and staff members who had worked at that school for the past 70 years! I learned that this old, high-maintenance, antiquated building was loved! I learned that I wasn't the only one who loved it; it was loved by generations.

Leadership Lesson #16

It is always important to celebrate. Celebrate the life of the building, the birthdays of your co-workers, the anniversaries of special events. It is way to show that you understand that you are part of history and the school is the central part of that history.

You are one of several, (or will be), leaders in that building's history. Your staff is the staff of the moment but you will find even when there is low turnover every year brings a different group dynamic and every year brings a different feel.

In the 8 years I was at Nokesville, I shook the hands of approximately 400 fifth graders on their last day of elementary school. That was more than the entire school held each year. I was the only principal they knew. However, there were 6 principals before me and 3 after me as of 2012.

Celebrate the history. You are part of it. It is important.

Chapter
17

It's Code Green You Have to Go In

Being located on the far western end of the county where you could see the Blue Ridge Mountains created a wonderful bucolic backdrop to that grand old brick building. It also created a traveling nightmare during the winter months.

When Prince William County received any measurable snowfall, there would usually receive much more in the western end of the county than the eastern end. There would be more snow in Nokesville than at the central office. The people at the central office would decide when there was heavy snow whether it would be Code Red (principals and head custodians do not need to report.) or Code Green (principals and head custodians had to come in or take leave.) If the snow was really bad, I would always pray that it would be a Code Red Day because if it was Code Green I would not take leave; I would go in.

The last winter I was there was one of the worst in my entire tenure. We had so much measurable snow that year that the teachers didn't finish their post planning days until right before the July 4th holiday. I remember driving home the Friday before July 4th and hearing from a radio announcer, "We are now half-way through the summer." I wanted to climb through the radio and hurt him. Anyway during a particularly snowy February, we were hammered with the kind of snow where we knew the kids would be off but the central office wasn't sure until between 5:00 a.m. and 6:00 a.m. the following morning whether I would be off.

They announced a Code Green.

I cleaned off my car and put on my snow gear. I did not dress up because nobody other than my Head Custodian was going to be there and certainly nobody from central office was coming by to help me shovel the sidewalks and check for roof leaks and make sure the boiler was still running. (Yes we had a boiler.)

The main roads were pretty good as long as you didn't try to go too fast and maintained your distance. The hour long drive only took about 20 minutes longer than usual and I was pretty confident as I drove down Fitzwater Drive and turned into the driveway. As I attempted to turn into my usual parking space it became clear to me that the car now had a mind of its own. It had responded to my wish to turn left but it would not stop when I stepped on the break. I was now making circles on an icy surface that had apparently not turned to water yet. I knew that I had to take my foot off the break and hands off the wheel and let it do what it wanted. I didn't have to worry about hitting anything because there was no one else and nothing else in the parking lot. (Because it was Code Green.) The car finally stopped gracefully between the fifth grade building and the playground equipment out in the far field! I quietly got out of the car, closed the door and walked up to the parking lot and kept walking through the 10 – 14 inches of snow until I reached the side door. I unlocked the door and entered the warm building.

About 10 minutes later, Mr. Herman, my head custodian came in and looked at me with a bemused look on his face and said, "Pretty interesting parking space you picked out today." I told him what happened. He said, "I didn't have any problem." I guess if I had waited 10 minutes the temperature would have been just high enough to keep me from having my own version of ice dancing in a car. Mr. Herman asked me if I wanted to move the car. I told him no I would take my chances at 4:00 p.m. (I got out fine.)

Several days later we received another measurable snow fall and a few days later another one. When we finally plowed the snow off the parking lot and toward the outdoor basketball court, the snow was tall enough for students to climb the mound and drop the basketball into the 8 foot basket.

Mr. Herman suggested that they add a Code Yellow to the Code Green and Code Red. I knew better than to ask but I did anyway. "What would be Code Yellow?" He replied, "To remind principals to be careful driving in their own parking lots."

Leadership Lesson #17

As a leader, you have to take the responsibility to go in and check on the building after a snow storm or other natural disaster. (Like a downdraft.) You have to go in because you know the building better than anyone else. You can tell in an instant if something isn't working or if there is a leak somewhere. You are the best person to clear the building and prepare it for students when all is clear and plowed.

Every area has its peculiarities. The north has snow. The south has hurricanes. The west has earthquakes. The Midwest has tornadoes. You have to know your area and know your school.

You can also learn how to drive in bad weather, run a plow and park your car wherever it leads you.

Chapter
18

There Was Some Learning Going On

As you have been reading the stories that I have shared about my eight years at Nokesville, you might have also been asking yourself, "Was there any learning going on? Did the teachers and kids master anything while all the other stuff was happening?"

Yes.

I had a great staff and they worked diligently to instruct the kids in reading and writing and math. It shouldn't be too surprising that a 70 year-old school would focus on the three R's. We had a mixed group of educators. We had young ones just starting out and older ones who came and never left. They worked hard to help students who had difficulty and who needed extra help. We had our usual number of special education students who were labeled autistic, learning disabled, developmentally delayed and speech impaired. We loved them all and helped them all.

I also started at Nokesville prior to the beginning of the accountability testing as it exists today. We had the Standards of Learning Tests in the Commonwealth of Virginia and we were used to analyzing how our kids faired in these yearly examinations. We did not have the need for every child in third and fifth grade to score a specific score to be promoted; that would come later in the new millennium. We did use the information learned from the testing to adjust our annual school plan and focus the following year's staff development.

In the years I was there, we added a phonics program, purchased math manipulatives and science lab materials. We constantly discussed how to improve students' writing and what to do with students who continually had difficulty. We had wonderfully active parents and some parents who drove us crazy. We always tried to do our best even if it sometimes didn't work.

In 8 years, we established a strong PTA and an active School Council that would survey our parents and our fifth graders to see how we could do a better job. I would spend hours in the classrooms every day and I would see good teaching and caring in most classes every day.

We did all of this at the same time we held walkathons and parades, supported circuses and local businesses, hosted Haunted Hallways and Talent Shows, and other fun things like dunk the principal or hit him with a pie if we read enough books.

I left Nokesville in June 2001. Nokesville was named a School of Excellence in the spring of 2002. The wonderful teachers and parents and students and community had earned it!

I was proud to have been part of it; 1/9 of it.

There was some learning going on even with all the fun stuff. Maybe that was part of the learning process too. Maybe that was part of what made us successful academically. Maybe that is what makes a great school!

Leadership Lesson #18

Never become so busy with the things that happen at school that you don't visit classrooms and speak to students and teachers and parents every day.

You will be surprised to find out that the majority of teachers in the world work very hard and want all their students to succeed. You will be surprised to find out that the majority of students want to behave and succeed. You will be surprised to find that the majority of parents will help their child and if you give suggestions they will try them.

Whenever I hear someone out in the community bash schools or the education system, I ask them a simple question: "When was the last time you visited a school?" They usually say they haven't.

I tell them to go visit any school they want and they will discover that there IS some learning going on.

Chapter 19

Thoughts On Leaving in 2001

It was apparent in 2001 that Patricia was not only considering retirement she was also getting all the paperwork together to make it happen. I was very supportive of her decision. I knew it was the right thing to do and that the timing was good for me to step away. Years later that decision was proven to be a blessing.

We decided that we would not mention it to anyone at Nokesville or at Patricia's school, Lake Ridge Middle, until we knew everything was signed and there was no turning back. Patricia had to complete the numerous documents needed to officially retire and I had to type of a letter of resignation effective June 30th 2001.

During this time as well, I was traveling down to Savannah in search of the next job to make equal money. I wasn't expecting more money just the same amount or so. We also had to find a house and be ready to move by the summer. We had friends who lived in Savannah who were kind enough to pick us up from the airport, show us houses for sale in the area and give us suggestions on companies to move us and drop me off at the Board of Education for several interviews.

In the summer of 2001, we did the hardest thing anyone ever agrees to do: Move to a new town, find a new job and move into a new house.

It wasn't as hard as saying goodbye.

I called a faculty meeting on a Monday afternoon in May and I asked Patricia to come with me. I calmly told the staff that Patricia was retiring and we had decided to move back to Savannah because we loved it there and it was where Patricia had started her teaching career back thirty years ago. I thanked the staff for the past 8 years. I thanked them for their dedication. I thanked them for teaching me how to be a principal. I thanked them for putting up with me at times. I thanked them for the fun and laughter and the long days and great times.

I cried.

As I have looked back on the Nokesville years, I can say it was one of the best times of my life. It was a lot of work but a rewarding experience. There were times when the upper echelon would be frustrated with me but we were doing things for the kids and for our community. It was a time when a 35 year old rookie principal learned how to be a leader from the greatest group of people I have ever known.

On June 30th 2001, I walked around and through the building one last time. I retraced my steps from 8 years earlier when I walked around looking through the windows. I went down into our storage room euphemistically called the dungeon. I walked through the upstairs rooms where we had so many haunted hallways. I was alone and that was fine with me.

I left the keys on my desk and closed the door one last time and walked to my car. With tears in my eyes, I rode around the building one final time and then proceeded on to the next part of my life. I blew the horn as I went passed the building; the building didn't respond.

Leadership Lesson #19

As you leave any job or leadership role, you should feel some sadness and the grief of parting. You have given your life to that job and you have loved that job. In the book, Leading With Soul, there is a line that has become my personal motto: "Work is love made visible." I have even put it on my school stationery. You have to love what you do and give it all the energy you can. You go in early and you stay late and you and your significant other attend community events because you realize you are a leader in the community.

It is a noble and wonderful job. I am glad that I was given the opportunity to be there for 8 years. In many ways, they were the hardest working years of my life. In many ways they were the best years of my life.

Chapter 20

Nokesville Since 2001

It has now been 10 years since I left Nokesville and there have been many changes for them and for me.

When Patricia and I came to Savannah, I was lucky enough to be hired by Savannah-Chatham County as the principal of Bloomingdale Elementary School. It is in the far western part of the county and it has its own police and fire departments and city council and mayor. (Sound familiar?) I have now been there ten years. It isn't Nokesville but Bloomingdale is a good place to be. It has dedicated teachers and good students and the same challenges that all schools have. We have been a passing school making Adequate Yearly Progress during the time I have been here. (Nokesville was good training.)

Nokesville itself has changed in 10 years. The building received a new roof in 2002. It is a bright green metal roof. I am sure the planes use it as a marker to land at Dulles International Airport. The nearby farms have been sold and they are building townhouses and single family homes where once the black angus and long horns roamed. They have widened the roads due to increased traffic. It is no longer the quiet bucolic place that it was. It still has the same beautiful view of the Blue Ridge.

The staff has changed as well. The principal that followed me was only there for two years. He retired and he was replaced by a principal who moved from a different county. So now it is an 82 year old building that has had 9 principals. Many of the staff has retired turning the reins over to younger professionals. Ms Lowe, (LP) has retired and Ms Harris who taught there for 42 years has also hung up her lanyard. Mr. Herman retired to North Carolina and Ms Cahill, my secretary has left to spend more time with her grandchildren. I believe that the new people will stay for a long time too. The area may change but the building still has good bones.

We lost several friends in the last 10 years. Peggy Beach, my wonderful PTA President who helped build our PTA, lost her daughter Katie in 2008 and then lost another daughter Alissa in 2010. Both kids grew up at Nokesville.

Both were only teenagers. I knew both very well and there is never a bigger loss to a family than losing a child.

In 2005, four years after coming to Savannah, Patricia was diagnosed with lung cancer. I now knew why it was important for her to retire and come back to Savannah and have some fun. She battled that awful disease for two years but died on February 12, 2007. It was the hardest thing I have ever had to endure and I learned that every day is precious and that your time is the greatest gift you can give to anyone.

I have with the help of a new lady in my life, Joy, found love and support and happiness that I have not know in several years. Joy certainly was named correctly. She has brought me out of the deepest sadness, loneliness and loss anyone can feel. I have been able to look back on those years and in 2011 feel able to write about my first years as a principal, my journey and my education.

Matthew, my oldest son, is now a Professor of philosophy at UCLA. (A doctor of philosophy, education does work.) Jason, my second son is now working for Google in San Francisco. They are both smart and take after their mother.

There are many things you don't learn in principal school. You have to see the dedication in the teachers you work with. You have to see the hardships some kids go through before they even get to school. You have to experience the way people come together to help a child, a family in need, or a community that wants to support its neighborhood school. You learn to cherish the days with the kids and cherish the days with your family and cherish the time that you have together. You realize that it all can end before you wanted it to; that your plans didn't turn out the way you thought it would be. You learn to be resilient and flexible and faithful and understanding. You learn that love really is the foundation of being successful in anything you do.

I learned to take the job seriously but not to take myself too seriously. I learned to take risks and be part of the community and be willing to do silly things if it was in the best interest of the students and the school.

I learned to be a principal. I learned to be a better man. I learned to keep learning and to persevere......and to laugh and love again.

It is the school and the faculty and the families and the students and the situations and the daily challenges that taught me to be a better principal and more importantly a better person. I thank them all for teaching me the stuff you don't learn in principal's school. It has been a great and wonderful ride; nothing like riding that elephant!